How To Use This Journal

The Lectio Divina is a 1,50~
of reading and meditating
It is a devotional prayei
comprised of 5 steps:

1. Silencio - Quiet your heart, slow down, and relax into God's presence.
2. Lectio - Read the scripture out loud, slowly and intentionally. Notice when a word or phrase sticks out to you and reflect on it. Listen and wait for God to speak
3. Meditatio - Meditate on the scripture, reading the scripture out loud again. Explore the invitation God is offering as you ponder the word or phrase.
4. Oratio - Respond, pray. Read a third time and pray, talking with God about what is highlighted.
5. Contemplatio - Contemplate in God's presence and allow time for the word or phrase to sink into your soul.

The Journal Prompts will help track the devotional, especially in steps 4 and 5.

Scripture Read: _____

What word or phrase sticks out to me?

_____

_____

What do I notice about how I feel when reading this word or phrase?

_____

_____

_____

What is the Holy Spirit speaking to me about this word or phrase?

_____

_____

_____

Where do I feel resistant to this word?

_____

_____

_____

How do I plan to continue to dwell on this today?

_____

_____

_____

Prayer:
Contemplation and rest in his presence
Share your feelings and resistance with God
Thank him for speaking to you

Scripture Read: _____

What word or phrase sticks out to me?

_____

_____

What do I notice about how I feel when reading this word or phrase?

_____

_____

_____

What is the Holy Spirit speaking to me about this word or phrase?

_____

_____

_____

Where do I feel resistant to this word?

_____

_____

_____

How do I plan to continue to dwell on this today?

_____

_____

_____

> Prayer:
> Contemplation and rest in his presence
> Share your feelings and resistance with God
> Thank him for speaking to you

Scripture Read: _____

What word or phrase sticks out to me?

_____

_____

What do I notice about how I feel when
reading this word or phrase?

_____

_____

_____

What is the Holy Spirit speaking to
me about this word or phrase?

_____

_____

_____

Where do I feel resistant to this word?

_____

_____

_____

How do I plan to continue to dwell on this today?

_____

_____

Prayer:
Contemplation and rest in his presence
Share your feelings and resistance with God
Thank him for speaking to you

Scripture Read: _____

What word or phrase sticks out to me?

_____
_____

What do I notice about how I feel when reading this word or phrase?

_____
_____

What is the Holy Spirit speaking to me about this word or phrase?

_____
_____

Where do I feel resistant to this word?

_____
_____

How do I plan to continue to dwell on this today?

_____
_____

Prayer:
Contemplation and rest in his presence
Share your feelings and resistance with God
Thank him for speaking to you

Scripture Read: _____

What word or phrase sticks out to me?

_____

_____

What do I notice about how I feel when
reading this word or phrase?

_____

_____

_____

What is the Holy Spirit speaking to
me about this word or phrase?

_____

_____

_____

Where do I feel resistant to this word?

_____

_____

_____

How do I plan to continue to dwell on this today?

_____

_____

Prayer:
Contemplation and rest in his presence
Share your feelings and resistance with God
Thank him for speaking to you

Scripture Read: _____

What word or phrase sticks out to me?

_____

_____

What do I notice about how I feel when
reading this word or phrase?

_____

_____

_____

What is the Holy Spirit speaking to
me about this word or phrase?

_____

_____

_____

Where do I feel resistant to this word?

_____

_____

_____

How do I plan to continue to dwell on this today?

_____

_____

_____

Prayer:
Contemplation and rest in his presence
Share your feelings and resistance with God
Thank him for speaking to you

Scripture Read: _____

What word or phrase sticks out to me?

_____
_____

What do I notice about how I feel when reading this word or phrase?

_____
_____
_____

What is the Holy Spirit speaking to me about this word or phrase?

_____
_____
_____

Where do I feel resistant to this word?

_____
_____

How do I plan to continue to dwell on this today?

_____
_____

Prayer:
Contemplation and rest in his presence
Share your feelings and resistance with God
Thank him for speaking to you

Scripture Read: _____

What word or phrase sticks out to me?

_____

_____

What do I notice about how I feel when
reading this word or phrase?

_____

_____

_____

What is the Holy Spirit speaking to
me about this word or phrase?

_____

_____

_____

Where do I feel resistant to this word?

_____

_____

_____

How do I plan to continue to dwell on this today?

_____

_____

Prayer:
Contemplation and rest in his presence
Share your feelings and resistance with God
Thank him for speaking to you

Scripture Read: _____

What word or phrase sticks out to me?

_____

_____

What do I notice about how I feel when reading this word or phrase?

_____

_____

What is the Holy Spirit speaking to me about this word or phrase?

_____

_____

Where do I feel resistant to this word?

_____

_____

How do I plan to continue to dwell on this today?

_____

Prayer:
Contemplation and rest in his presence
Share your feelings and resistance with God
Thank him for speaking to you

Scripture Read: _____

What word or phrase sticks out to me?

_____

_____

What do I notice about how I feel when
reading this word or phrase?

_____

_____

_____

What is the Holy Spirit speaking to
me about this word or phrase?

_____

_____

_____

Where do I feel resistant to this word?

_____

_____

_____

How do I plan to continue to dwell on this today?

_____

_____

Prayer:
Contemplation and rest in his presence
Share your feelings and resistance with God
Thank him for speaking to you

Scripture Read: _____

What word or phrase sticks out to me?

_____

_____

What do I notice about how I feel when
reading this word or phrase?

_____

_____

What is the Holy Spirit speaking to
me about this word or phrase?

_____

_____

Where do I feel resistant to this word?

_____

_____

How do I plan to continue to dwell on this today?

_____

_____

Prayer:
Contemplation and rest in his presence
Share your feelings and resistance with God
Thank him for speaking to you

Scripture Read: _____

What word or phrase sticks out to me?

_____

_____

What do I notice about how I feel when
reading this word or phrase?

_____

_____

_____

What is the Holy Spirit speaking to
me about this word or phrase?

_____

_____

_____

Where do I feel resistant to this word?

_____

_____

_____

How do I plan to continue to dwell on this today?

_____

_____

Prayer:
Contemplation and rest in his presence
Share your feelings and resistance with God
Thank him for speaking to you

Scripture Read: _____

What word or phrase sticks out to me?

_____

_____

What do I notice about how I feel when
reading this word or phrase?

_____

_____

_____

What is the Holy Spirit speaking to
me about this word or phrase?

_____

_____

_____

Where do I feel resistant to this word?

_____

_____

_____

How do I plan to continue to dwell on this today?

_____

_____

Prayer:
Contemplation and rest in his presence
Share your feelings and resistance with God
Thank him for speaking to you

Scripture Read: _____

What word or phrase sticks out to me?

_____

_____

What do I notice about how I feel when
reading this word or phrase?

_____

_____

_____

What is the Holy Spirit speaking to
me about this word or phrase?

_____

_____

_____

Where do I feel resistant to this word?

_____

_____

_____

How do I plan to continue to dwell on this today?

_____

_____

Prayer:
Contemplation and rest in his presence
Share your feelings and resistance with God
Thank him for speaking to you

Scripture Read: _____

What word or phrase sticks out to me?

_____

What do I notice about how I feel when
reading this word or phrase?

_____

_____

What is the Holy Spirit speaking to
me about this word or phrase?

_____

_____

Where do I feel resistant to this word?

_____

_____

How do I plan to continue to dwell on this today?

_____

_____

Prayer:
Contemplation and rest in his presence
Share your feelings and resistance with God
Thank him for speaking to you

Scripture Read: _____

What word or phrase sticks out to me?

_____

_____

What do I notice about how I feel when reading this word or phrase?

_____

_____

What is the Holy Spirit speaking to me about this word or phrase?

_____

_____

Where do I feel resistant to this word?

_____

_____

How do I plan to continue to dwell on this today?

_____

Prayer:
Contemplation and rest in his presence
Share your feelings and resistance with God
Thank him for speaking to you

Scripture Read: _____

What word or phrase sticks out to me?

_____
_____

What do I notice about how I feel when
reading this word or phrase?

_____
_____
_____

What is the Holy Spirit speaking to
me about this word or phrase?

_____
_____
_____

Where do I feel resistant to this word?

_____
_____
_____

How do I plan to continue to dwell on this today?

_____
_____

Prayer:
Contemplation and rest in his presence
Share your feelings and resistance with God
Thank him for speaking to you

Scripture Read: _____

What word or phrase sticks out to me?

_____

_____

What do I notice about how I feel when
reading this word or phrase?

_____

_____

What is the Holy Spirit speaking to
me about this word or phrase?

_____

_____

Where do I feel resistant to this word?

_____

_____

How do I plan to continue to dwell on this today?

_____

_____

Prayer:
Contemplation and rest in his presence
Share your feelings and resistance with God
Thank him for speaking to you

Scripture Read: _____

What word or phrase sticks out to me?

_____

_____

What do I notice about how I feel when reading this word or phrase?

_____

_____

_____

What is the Holy Spirit speaking to me about this word or phrase?

_____

_____

_____

Where do I feel resistant to this word?

_____

_____

_____

How do I plan to continue to dwell on this today?

_____

_____

Prayer:
Contemplation and rest in his presence
Share your feelings and resistance with God
Thank him for speaking to you

Scripture Read: _____

What word or phrase sticks out to me?

_____

_____

What do I notice about how I feel when reading this word or phrase?

_____

_____

_____

What is the Holy Spirit speaking to me about this word or phrase?

_____

_____

_____

Where do I feel resistant to this word?

_____

_____

_____

How do I plan to continue to dwell on this today?

_____

_____

Prayer:
Contemplation and rest in his presence
Share your feelings and resistance with God
Thank him for speaking to you

Scripture Read: _____

What word or phrase sticks out to me?

_____

_____

What do I notice about how I feel when
reading this word or phrase?

_____

_____

_____

What is the Holy Spirit speaking to
me about this word or phrase?

_____

_____

_____

Where do I feel resistant to this word?

_____

_____

_____

How do I plan to continue to dwell on this today?

_____

_____

Prayer:
Contemplation and rest in his presence
Share your feelings and resistance with God
Thank him for speaking to you

Scripture Read: _____

What word or phrase sticks out to me?

_____

_____

What do I notice about how I feel when
reading this word or phrase?

_____

_____

_____

What is the Holy Spirit speaking to
me about this word or phrase?

_____

_____

_____

Where do I feel resistant to this word?

_____

_____

How do I plan to continue to dwell on this today?

_____

_____

Prayer:
Contemplation and rest in his presence
Share your feelings and resistance with God
Thank him for speaking to you

Scripture Read: _____

What word or phrase sticks out to me?

_____
_____

What do I notice about how I feel when reading this word or phrase?

_____
_____
_____

What is the Holy Spirit speaking to me about this word or phrase?

_____
_____
_____

Where do I feel resistant to this word?

_____
_____
_____

How do I plan to continue to dwell on this today?

_____
_____

Prayer:
Contemplation and rest in his presence
Share your feelings and resistance with God
Thank him for speaking to you

Scripture Read: _____

What word or phrase sticks out to me?

_____

_____

What do I notice about how I feel when
reading this word or phrase?

_____

_____

What is the Holy Spirit speaking to
me about this word or phrase?

_____

_____

Where do I feel resistant to this word?

_____

_____

How do I plan to continue to dwell on this today?

_____

_____

Prayer:
Contemplation and rest in his presence
Share your feelings and resistance with God
Thank him for speaking to you

Scripture Read: _____

What word or phrase sticks out to me?

_____

_____

What do I notice about how I feel when reading this word or phrase?

_____

_____

_____

What is the Holy Spirit speaking to me about this word or phrase?

_____

_____

_____

Where do I feel resistant to this word?

_____

_____

_____

How do I plan to continue to dwell on this today?

_____

_____

Prayer:
Contemplation and rest in his presence
Share your feelings and resistance with God
Thank him for speaking to you

Scripture Read: _____

What word or phrase sticks out to me?

_____
_____

What do I notice about how I feel when
reading this word or phrase?

_____
_____
_____

What is the Holy Spirit speaking to
me about this word or phrase?

_____
_____
_____

Where do I feel resistant to this word?

_____
_____
_____

How do I plan to continue to dwell on this today?

_____
_____

Prayer:
Contemplation and rest in his presence
Share your feelings and resistance with God
Thank him for speaking to you

Scripture Read: _____

What word or phrase sticks out to me?

_____

_____

What do I notice about how I feel when reading this word or phrase?

_____

_____

_____

What is the Holy Spirit speaking to me about this word or phrase?

_____

_____

_____

Where do I feel resistant to this word?

_____

_____

_____

How do I plan to continue to dwell on this today?

_____

_____

Prayer:
Contemplation and rest in his presence
Share your feelings and resistance with God
Thank him for speaking to you

Scripture Read: _____

What word or phrase sticks out to me?

_____

_____

What do I notice about how I feel when
reading this word or phrase?

_____

_____

_____

What is the Holy Spirit speaking to
me about this word or phrase?

_____

_____

_____

Where do I feel resistant to this word?

_____

_____

_____

How do I plan to continue to dwell on this today?

_____

_____

Prayer:
Contemplation and rest in his presence
Share your feelings and resistance with God
Thank him for speaking to you

Scripture Read: _____

What word or phrase sticks out to me?

_____

_____

What do I notice about how I feel when
reading this word or phrase?

_____

_____

_____

What is the Holy Spirit speaking to
me about this word or phrase?

_____

_____

_____

Where do I feel resistant to this word?

_____

_____

_____

How do I plan to continue to dwell on this today?

_____

_____

Prayer:
Contemplation and rest in his presence
Share your feelings and resistance with God
Thank him for speaking to you

Scripture Read: _____

What word or phrase sticks out to me?

_____

_____

What do I notice about how I feel when reading this word or phrase?

_____

_____

_____

What is the Holy Spirit speaking to me about this word or phrase?

_____

_____

_____

Where do I feel resistant to this word?

_____

_____

_____

How do I plan to continue to dwell on this today?

_____

_____

Prayer:
Contemplation and rest in his presence
Share your feelings and resistance with God
Thank him for speaking to you

Scripture Read: _____

What word or phrase sticks out to me?

_____
_____

What do I notice about how I feel when
reading this word or phrase?

_____
_____
_____

What is the Holy Spirit speaking to
me about this word or phrase?

_____
_____
_____

Where do I feel resistant to this word?

_____
_____
_____

How do I plan to continue to dwell on this today?

_____
_____

Prayer:
Contemplation and rest in his presence
Share your feelings and resistance with God
Thank him for speaking to you

Scripture Read: _____

What word or phrase sticks out to me?

_____

_____

What do I notice about how I feel when
reading this word or phrase?

_____

_____

_____

What is the Holy Spirit speaking to
me about this word or phrase?

_____

_____

Where do I feel resistant to this word?

_____

_____

How do I plan to continue to dwell on this today?

_____

_____

Prayer:
Contemplation and rest in his presence
Share your feelings and resistance with God
Thank him for speaking to you

Scripture Read: _____

What word or phrase sticks out to me?

_____
_____

What do I notice about how I feel when reading this word or phrase?

_____
_____
_____

What is the Holy Spirit speaking to me about this word or phrase?

_____
_____
_____

Where do I feel resistant to this word?

_____
_____
_____

How do I plan to continue to dwell on this today?

_____
_____

Prayer:
Contemplation and rest in his presence
Share your feelings and resistance with God
Thank him for speaking to you

Scripture Read: _____

What word or phrase sticks out to me?

_____

_____

What do I notice about how I feel when
reading this word or phrase?

_____

_____

What is the Holy Spirit speaking to
me about this word or phrase?

_____

_____

Where do I feel resistant to this word?

_____

_____

How do I plan to continue to dwell on this today?

_____

Prayer:
Contemplation and rest in his presence
Share your feelings and resistance with God
Thank him for speaking to you

Scripture Read: _____

What word or phrase sticks out to me?

_____

_____

What do I notice about how I feel when
reading this word or phrase?

_____

_____

_____

What is the Holy Spirit speaking to
me about this word or phrase?

_____

_____

_____

Where do I feel resistant to this word?

_____

_____

_____

How do I plan to continue to dwell on this today?

_____

_____

Prayer:
Contemplation and rest in his presence
Share your feelings and resistance with God
Thank him for speaking to you

Scripture Read: _____

What word or phrase sticks out to me?

_____

_____

What do I notice about how I feel when
reading this word or phrase?

_____

_____

_____

What is the Holy Spirit speaking to
me about this word or phrase?

_____

_____

_____

Where do I feel resistant to this word?

_____

_____

_____

How do I plan to continue to dwell on this today?

_____

_____

Prayer:
Contemplation and rest in his presence
Share your feelings and resistance with God
Thank him for speaking to you

Scripture Read: _____

What word or phrase sticks out to me?

_____

_____

What do I notice about how I feel when reading this word or phrase?

_____

_____

_____

What is the Holy Spirit speaking to me about this word or phrase?

_____

_____

_____

Where do I feel resistant to this word?

_____

_____

_____

How do I plan to continue to dwell on this today?

_____

_____

Prayer:
Contemplation and rest in his presence
Share your feelings and resistance with God
Thank him for speaking to you

Scripture Read: _____

What word or phrase sticks out to me?

_____

_____

What do I notice about how I feel when reading this word or phrase?

_____

_____

What is the Holy Spirit speaking to me about this word or phrase?

_____

_____

Where do I feel resistant to this word?

_____

_____

How do I plan to continue to dwell on this today?

_____

_____

Prayer:

Contemplation and rest in his presence

Share your feelings and resistance with God

Thank him for speaking to you

Scripture Read: _____

What word or phrase sticks out to me?

_____

_____

What do I notice about how I feel when reading this word or phrase?

_____

_____

_____

What is the Holy Spirit speaking to me about this word or phrase?

_____

_____

_____

Where do I feel resistant to this word?

_____

_____

How do I plan to continue to dwell on this today?

_____

_____

Prayer:
Contemplation and rest in his presence
Share your feelings and resistance with God
Thank him for speaking to you

Scripture Read: _____

What word or phrase sticks out to me?

_____

_____

What do I notice about how I feel when
reading this word or phrase?

_____

_____

What is the Holy Spirit speaking to
me about this word or phrase?

_____

_____

Where do I feel resistant to this word?

_____

_____

How do I plan to continue to dwell on this today?

_____

_____

Prayer:
Contemplation and rest in his presence
Share your feelings and resistance with God
Thank him for speaking to you

Scripture Read: _____

What word or phrase sticks out to me?

_____

_____

What do I notice about how I feel when reading this word or phrase?

_____

_____

_____

What is the Holy Spirit speaking to me about this word or phrase?

_____

_____

_____

Where do I feel resistant to this word?

_____

_____

_____

How do I plan to continue to dwell on this today?

_____

_____

_____

Prayer:
Contemplation and rest in his presence
Share your feelings and resistance with God
Thank him for speaking to you

Scripture Read: _____

What word or phrase sticks out to me?

_____

_____

What do I notice about how I feel when
reading this word or phrase?

_____

_____

_____

What is the Holy Spirit speaking to
me about this word or phrase?

_____

_____

_____

Where do I feel resistant to this word?

_____

_____

_____

How do I plan to continue to dwell on this today?

_____

_____

Prayer:
Contemplation and rest in his presence
Share your feelings and resistance with God
Thank him for speaking to you

Scripture Read: _____

What word or phrase sticks out to me?

_____

_____

What do I notice about how I feel when reading this word or phrase?

_____

_____

_____

What is the Holy Spirit speaking to me about this word or phrase?

_____

_____

_____

Where do I feel resistant to this word?

_____

_____

_____

How do I plan to continue to dwell on this today?

_____

_____

Prayer:
Contemplation and rest in his presence
Share your feelings and resistance with God
Thank him for speaking to you

Scripture Read: _____

What word or phrase sticks out to me?

_____

_____

What do I notice about how I feel when reading this word or phrase?

_____

_____

_____

What is the Holy Spirit speaking to me about this word or phrase?

_____

_____

_____

Where do I feel resistant to this word?

_____

_____

_____

How do I plan to continue to dwell on this today?

_____

_____

Prayer:
Contemplation and rest in his presence
Share your feelings and resistance with God
Thank him for speaking to you

Scripture Read: _____

What word or phrase sticks out to me?

_____

_____

What do I notice about how I feel when
reading this word or phrase?

_____

_____

_____

What is the Holy Spirit speaking to
me about this word or phrase?

_____

_____

_____

Where do I feel resistant to this word?

_____

_____

_____

How do I plan to continue to dwell on this today?

_____

_____

Prayer:
Contemplation and rest in his presence
Share your feelings and resistance with God
Thank him for speaking to you

Scripture Read: _____

What word or phrase sticks out to me?

_____

_____

What do I notice about how I feel when
reading this word or phrase?

_____

_____

_____

What is the Holy Spirit speaking to
me about this word or phrase?

_____

_____

_____

Where do I feel resistant to this word?

_____

_____

_____

How do I plan to continue to dwell on this today?

_____

_____

_____

Prayer:
Contemplation and rest in his presence
Share your feelings and resistance with God
Thank him for speaking to you

Scripture Read: _____

What word or phrase sticks out to me?

_____

_____

What do I notice about how I feel when
reading this word or phrase?

_____

_____

_____

What is the Holy Spirit speaking to
me about this word or phrase?

_____

_____

_____

Where do I feel resistant to this word?

_____

_____

_____

How do I plan to continue to dwell on this today?

_____

_____

Prayer:
Contemplation and rest in his presence
Share your feelings and resistance with God
Thank him for speaking to you

Scripture Read: _____

What word or phrase sticks out to me?

_____

_____

What do I notice about how I feel when reading this word or phrase?

_____

_____

_____

What is the Holy Spirit speaking to me about this word or phrase?

_____

_____

Where do I feel resistant to this word?

_____

_____

How do I plan to continue to dwell on this today?

_____

_____

Prayer:
Contemplation and rest in his presence
Share your feelings and resistance with God
Thank him for speaking to you

Scripture Read: _____

What word or phrase sticks out to me?

_____

_____

What do I notice about how I feel when
reading this word or phrase?

_____

_____

_____

What is the Holy Spirit speaking to
me about this word or phrase?

_____

_____

_____

Where do I feel resistant to this word?

_____

_____

_____

How do I plan to continue to dwell on this today?

_____

_____

Prayer:
Contemplation and rest in his presence
Share your feelings and resistance with God
Thank him for speaking to you

Scripture Read: _____

What word or phrase sticks out to me?

_____

_____

What do I notice about how I feel when reading this word or phrase?

_____

_____

_____

What is the Holy Spirit speaking to me about this word or phrase?

_____

_____

Where do I feel resistant to this word?

_____

_____

How do I plan to continue to dwell on this today?

_____

_____

Prayer:
Contemplation and rest in his presence
Share your feelings and resistance with God
Thank him for speaking to you

Scripture Read: _____

What word or phrase sticks out to me?

_____

_____

What do I notice about how I feel when reading this word or phrase?

_____

_____

_____

What is the Holy Spirit speaking to me about this word or phrase?

_____

_____

_____

Where do I feel resistant to this word?

_____

_____

_____

How do I plan to continue to dwell on this today?

_____

_____

Prayer:
Contemplation and rest in his presence
Share your feelings and resistance with God
Thank him for speaking to you

Scripture Read: _____

What word or phrase sticks out to me?

_____

_____

What do I notice about how I feel when reading this word or phrase?

_____

_____

_____

_____

What is the Holy Spirit speaking to me about this word or phrase?

_____

_____

_____

Where do I feel resistant to this word?

_____

_____

_____

How do I plan to continue to dwell on this today?

_____

_____

Prayer:
Contemplation and rest in his presence
Share your feelings and resistance with God
Thank him for speaking to you

Scripture Read: _____

What word or phrase sticks out to me?

_____
_____

What do I notice about how I feel when reading this word or phrase?

_____
_____
_____

What is the Holy Spirit speaking to me about this word or phrase?

_____
_____
_____

Where do I feel resistant to this word?

_____
_____
_____

How do I plan to continue to dwell on this today?

_____
_____

Prayer:
Contemplation and rest in his presence
Share your feelings and resistance with God
Thank him for speaking to you

Scripture Read: _____

What word or phrase sticks out to me?

_____

_____

What do I notice about how I feel when reading this word or phrase?

_____

_____

_____

What is the Holy Spirit speaking to me about this word or phrase?

_____

_____

_____

Where do I feel resistant to this word?

_____

_____

_____

How do I plan to continue to dwell on this today?

_____

_____

Prayer:
Contemplation and rest in his presence
Share your feelings and resistance with God
Thank him for speaking to you

Scripture Read: _____

What word or phrase sticks out to me?

_____

_____

What do I notice about how I feel when reading this word or phrase?

_____

_____

_____

What is the Holy Spirit speaking to me about this word or phrase?

_____

_____

_____

Where do I feel resistant to this word?

_____

_____

_____

How do I plan to continue to dwell on this today?

_____

Prayer:
Contemplation and rest in his presence
Share your feelings and resistance with God
Thank him for speaking to you

Scripture Read: _____

What word or phrase sticks out to me?

_____

_____

What do I notice about how I feel when reading this word or phrase?

_____

_____

_____

What is the Holy Spirit speaking to me about this word or phrase?

_____

_____

_____

Where do I feel resistant to this word?

_____

_____

_____

How do I plan to continue to dwell on this today?

_____

_____

_____

Prayer:
Contemplation and rest in his presence
Share your feelings and resistance with God
Thank him for speaking to you

Scripture Read: _____

What word or phrase sticks out to me?

_____
_____

What do I notice about how I feel when
reading this word or phrase?

_____
_____
_____

What is the Holy Spirit speaking to
me about this word or phrase?

_____
_____
_____

Where do I feel resistant to this word?

_____
_____
_____

How do I plan to continue to dwell on this today?

_____
_____

Prayer:
Contemplation and rest in his presence
Share your feelings and resistance with God
Thank him for speaking to you

Scripture Read: _____

What word or phrase sticks out to me?

_____

_____

What do I notice about how I feel when
reading this word or phrase?

_____

_____

What is the Holy Spirit speaking to
me about this word or phrase?

_____

_____

Where do I feel resistant to this word?

_____

_____

How do I plan to continue to dwell on this today?

_____

Prayer:
Contemplation and rest in his presence
Share your feelings and resistance with God
Thank him for speaking to you

Scripture Read: _____

What word or phrase sticks out to me?

_____

_____

What do I notice about how I feel when reading this word or phrase?

_____

_____

_____

What is the Holy Spirit speaking to me about this word or phrase?

_____

_____

_____

Where do I feel resistant to this word?

_____

_____

_____

How do I plan to continue to dwell on this today?

_____

_____

Prayer:
Contemplation and rest in his presence
Share your feelings and resistance with God
Thank him for speaking to you

Scripture Read: _____

What word or phrase sticks out to me?

_____

_____

What do I notice about how I feel when
reading this word or phrase?

_____

_____

_____

What is the Holy Spirit speaking to
me about this word or phrase?

_____

_____

_____

Where do I feel resistant to this word?

_____

_____

_____

How do I plan to continue to dwell on this today?

_____

_____

Prayer:
Contemplation and rest in his presence
Share your feelings and resistance with God
Thank him for speaking to you

Scripture Read: _____

What word or phrase sticks out to me?

_____

_____

What do I notice about how I feel when reading this word or phrase?

_____

_____

_____

What is the Holy Spirit speaking to me about this word or phrase?

_____

_____

_____

Where do I feel resistant to this word?

_____

_____

_____

How do I plan to continue to dwell on this today?

_____

_____

_____

Prayer:
Contemplation and rest in his presence
Share your feelings and resistance with God
Thank him for speaking to you

Scripture Read: _____

What word or phrase sticks out to me?

_____

_____

What do I notice about how I feel when reading this word or phrase?

_____

_____

What is the Holy Spirit speaking to me about this word or phrase?

_____

_____

Where do I feel resistant to this word?

_____

_____

How do I plan to continue to dwell on this today?

_____

_____

Prayer:
Contemplation and rest in his presence
Share your feelings and resistance with God
Thank him for speaking to you

Scripture Read: _____

What word or phrase sticks out to me?

_____

_____

What do I notice about how I feel when reading this word or phrase?

_____

_____

_____

What is the Holy Spirit speaking to me about this word or phrase?

_____

_____

_____

Where do I feel resistant to this word?

_____

_____

_____

How do I plan to continue to dwell on this today?

_____

_____

Prayer:
Contemplation and rest in his presence
Share your feelings and resistance with God
Thank him for speaking to you

Scripture Read: _____

What word or phrase sticks out to me?

_____

_____

What do I notice about how I feel when
reading this word or phrase?

_____

_____

_____

What is the Holy Spirit speaking to
me about this word or phrase?

_____

_____

_____

Where do I feel resistant to this word?

_____

_____

_____

How do I plan to continue to dwell on this today?

_____

_____

Prayer:
Contemplation and rest in his presence
Share your feelings and resistance with God
Thank him for speaking to you

Scripture Read: _____

What word or phrase sticks out to me?

_____

_____

What do I notice about how I feel when reading this word or phrase?

_____

_____

_____

What is the Holy Spirit speaking to me about this word or phrase?

_____

_____

_____

Where do I feel resistant to this word?

_____

_____

_____

How do I plan to continue to dwell on this today?

_____

_____

Prayer:
Contemplation and rest in his presence
Share your feelings and resistance with God
Thank him for speaking to you

Scripture Read: _____

What word or phrase sticks out to me?

_____

_____

What do I notice about how I feel when
reading this word or phrase?

_____

_____

_____

What is the Holy Spirit speaking to
me about this word or phrase?

_____

_____

_____

Where do I feel resistant to this word?

_____

_____

How do I plan to continue to dwell on this today?

_____

_____

Prayer:
Contemplation and rest in his presence
Share your feelings and resistance with God
Thank him for speaking to you

Scripture Read: _____

What word or phrase sticks out to me?

_____

_____

What do I notice about how I feel when
reading this word or phrase?

_____

_____

_____

What is the Holy Spirit speaking to
me about this word or phrase?

_____

_____

Where do I feel resistant to this word?

_____

_____

How do I plan to continue to dwell on this today?

_____

_____

Prayer:
Contemplation and rest in his presence
Share your feelings and resistance with God
Thank him for speaking to you

Scripture Read: _____

What word or phrase sticks out to me?

_____

_____

What do I notice about how I feel when reading this word or phrase?

_____

_____

_____

What is the Holy Spirit speaking to me about this word or phrase?

_____

_____

_____

Where do I feel resistant to this word?

_____

_____

_____

How do I plan to continue to dwell on this today?

_____

_____

Prayer:
Contemplation and rest in his presence
Share your feelings and resistance with God
Thank him for speaking to you

Scripture Read: _____

What word or phrase sticks out to me?

_____

_____

What do I notice about how I feel when reading this word or phrase?

_____

_____

_____

What is the Holy Spirit speaking to me about this word or phrase?

_____

_____

_____

Where do I feel resistant to this word?

_____

_____

_____

How do I plan to continue to dwell on this today?

_____

_____

Prayer:
Contemplation and rest in his presence
Share your feelings and resistance with God
Thank him for speaking to you

Scripture Read: _____

What word or phrase sticks out to me?

_____

_____

What do I notice about how I feel when
reading this word or phrase?

_____

_____

_____

What is the Holy Spirit speaking to
me about this word or phrase?

_____

_____

_____

Where do I feel resistant to this word?

_____

_____

_____

How do I plan to continue to dwell on this today?

_____

_____

Prayer:
Contemplation and rest in his presence
Share your feelings and resistance with God
Thank him for speaking to you

Scripture Read: _____

What word or phrase sticks out to me?

_____

_____

What do I notice about how I feel when reading this word or phrase?

_____

_____

What is the Holy Spirit speaking to me about this word or phrase?

_____

_____

Where do I feel resistant to this word?

_____

_____

How do I plan to continue to dwell on this today?

_____

_____

Prayer:
Contemplation and rest in his presence
Share your feelings and resistance with God
Thank him for speaking to you

Scripture Read: _____

What word or phrase sticks out to me?

_____

_____

What do I notice about how I feel when
reading this word or phrase?

_____

_____

_____

What is the Holy Spirit speaking to
me about this word or phrase?

_____

_____

_____

Where do I feel resistant to this word?

_____

_____

How do I plan to continue to dwell on this today?

_____

_____

Prayer:
Contemplation and rest in his presence
Share your feelings and resistance with God
Thank him for speaking to you

Scripture Read: _____

What word or phrase sticks out to me?

_____

_____

What do I notice about how I feel when reading this word or phrase?

_____

_____

_____

What is the Holy Spirit speaking to me about this word or phrase?

_____

_____

Where do I feel resistant to this word?

_____

_____

How do I plan to continue to dwell on this today?

_____

_____

Prayer:
Contemplation and rest in his presence
Share your feelings and resistance with God
Thank him for speaking to you

Scripture Read: _____

What word or phrase sticks out to me?

_____

_____

What do I notice about how I feel when
reading this word or phrase?

_____

_____

_____

What is the Holy Spirit speaking to
me about this word or phrase?

_____

_____

_____

Where do I feel resistant to this word?

_____

_____

_____

How do I plan to continue to dwell on this today?

_____

_____

Prayer:
Contemplation and rest in his presence
Share your feelings and resistance with God
Thank him for speaking to you

Scripture Read: _____

What word or phrase sticks out to me?

_____

_____

What do I notice about how I feel when reading this word or phrase?

_____

_____

_____

What is the Holy Spirit speaking to me about this word or phrase?

_____

_____

_____

Where do I feel resistant to this word?

_____

_____

_____

How do I plan to continue to dwell on this today?

_____

_____

Prayer:
Contemplation and rest in his presence
Share your feelings and resistance with God
Thank him for speaking to you

Scripture Read: _____

What word or phrase sticks out to me?

_____

_____

What do I notice about how I feel when
reading this word or phrase?

_____

_____

_____

What is the Holy Spirit speaking to
me about this word or phrase?

_____

_____

_____

Where do I feel resistant to this word?

_____

_____

_____

How do I plan to continue to dwell on this today?

_____

_____

Prayer:
Contemplation and rest in his presence
Share your feelings and resistance with God
Thank him for speaking to you

Scripture Read: _____

What word or phrase sticks out to me?

_____
_____

What do I notice about how I feel when reading this word or phrase?

_____
_____
_____

What is the Holy Spirit speaking to me about this word or phrase?

_____
_____
_____

Where do I feel resistant to this word?

_____
_____
_____

How do I plan to continue to dwell on this today?

_____
_____

Prayer:
Contemplation and rest in his presence
Share your feelings and resistance with God
Thank him for speaking to you

Scripture Read: _____

What word or phrase sticks out to me?

_____
_____

What do I notice about how I feel when
reading this word or phrase?

_____
_____
_____

What is the Holy Spirit speaking to
me about this word or phrase?

_____
_____
_____

Where do I feel resistant to this word?

_____
_____
_____

How do I plan to continue to dwell on this today?

_____
_____

Prayer:
Contemplation and rest in his presence
Share your feelings and resistance with God
Thank him for speaking to you

Scripture Read: _____

What word or phrase sticks out to me?

_____

_____

What do I notice about how I feel when reading this word or phrase?

_____

_____

_____

What is the Holy Spirit speaking to me about this word or phrase?

_____

_____

_____

Where do I feel resistant to this word?

_____

_____

_____

How do I plan to continue to dwell on this today?

_____

_____

Prayer:
Contemplation and rest in his presence
Share your feelings and resistance with God
Thank him for speaking to you

Scripture Read: _____

What word or phrase sticks out to me?

_____

_____

What do I notice about how I feel when
reading this word or phrase?

_____

_____

_____

What is the Holy Spirit speaking to
me about this word or phrase?

_____

_____

_____

Where do I feel resistant to this word?

_____

_____

_____

How do I plan to continue to dwell on this today?

_____

_____

```
Prayer:
Contemplation and rest in his presence
Share your feelings and resistance with God
Thank him for speaking to you
```

Scripture Read: _____

What word or phrase sticks out to me?

_____

_____

What do I notice about how I feel when
reading this word or phrase?

_____

_____

What is the Holy Spirit speaking to
me about this word or phrase?

_____

_____

Where do I feel resistant to this word?

_____

_____

How do I plan to continue to dwell on this today?

_____

_____

Prayer:
Contemplation and rest in his presence
Share your feelings and resistance with God
Thank him for speaking to you

Scripture Read: _____

What word or phrase sticks out to me?

_____
_____

What do I notice about how I feel when
reading this word or phrase?

_____
_____
_____

What is the Holy Spirit speaking to
me about this word or phrase?

_____
_____
_____

Where do I feel resistant to this word?

_____
_____
_____

How do I plan to continue to dwell on this today?

_____
_____

Prayer:
Contemplation and rest in his presence
Share your feelings and resistance with God
Thank him for speaking to you

Scripture Read: _____

What word or phrase sticks out to me?

_____

_____

What do I notice about how I feel when reading this word or phrase?

_____

_____

_____

What is the Holy Spirit speaking to me about this word or phrase?

_____

_____

_____

Where do I feel resistant to this word?

_____

_____

_____

How do I plan to continue to dwell on this today?

_____

_____

Prayer:
Contemplation and rest in his presence
Share your feelings and resistance with God
Thank him for speaking to you

Scripture Read: _____

What word or phrase sticks out to me?

_____
_____

What do I notice about how I feel when
reading this word or phrase?

_____
_____
_____

What is the Holy Spirit speaking to
me about this word or phrase?

_____
_____
_____

Where do I feel resistant to this word?

_____
_____

How do I plan to continue to dwell on this today?

_____
_____

Prayer:
Contemplation and rest in his presence
Share your feelings and resistance with God
Thank him for speaking to you

Scripture Read: _____

What word or phrase sticks out to me?

_____
_____

What do I notice about how I feel when reading this word or phrase?

_____
_____
_____

What is the Holy Spirit speaking to me about this word or phrase?

_____
_____
_____

Where do I feel resistant to this word?

_____
_____
_____

How do I plan to continue to dwell on this today?

_____
_____
_____

Prayer:
Contemplation and rest in his presence
Share your feelings and resistance with God
Thank him for speaking to you

Scripture Read: _____

What word or phrase sticks out to me?

_____

_____

What do I notice about how I feel when
reading this word or phrase?

_____

_____

_____

What is the Holy Spirit speaking to
me about this word or phrase?

_____

_____

_____

Where do I feel resistant to this word?

_____

_____

How do I plan to continue to dwell on this today?

_____

_____

Prayer:
Contemplation and rest in his presence
Share your feelings and resistance with God
Thank him for speaking to you

Scripture Read: _____

What word or phrase sticks out to me?

_____

_____

What do I notice about how I feel when reading this word or phrase?

_____

_____

_____

What is the Holy Spirit speaking to me about this word or phrase?

_____

_____

_____

Where do I feel resistant to this word?

_____

_____

_____

How do I plan to continue to dwell on this today?

_____

_____

Prayer:
Contemplation and rest in his presence
Share your feelings and resistance with God
Thank him for speaking to you

Scripture Read: _____

What word or phrase sticks out to me?

_____
_____

What do I notice about how I feel when
reading this word or phrase?

_____
_____
_____

What is the Holy Spirit speaking to
me about this word or phrase?

_____
_____
_____

Where do I feel resistant to this word?

_____
_____

How do I plan to continue to dwell on this today?

_____
_____

Prayer:
Contemplation and rest in his presence
Share your feelings and resistance with God
Thank him for speaking to you

Scripture Read: _____

What word or phrase sticks out to me?

_____

_____

What do I notice about how I feel when reading this word or phrase?

_____

_____

_____

What is the Holy Spirit speaking to me about this word or phrase?

_____

_____

_____

Where do I feel resistant to this word?

_____

_____

_____

How do I plan to continue to dwell on this today?

_____

_____

_____

Prayer:
Contemplation and rest in his presence
Share your feelings and resistance with God
Thank him for speaking to you

Scripture Read: _____

What word or phrase sticks out to me?

_____

_____

What do I notice about how I feel when
reading this word or phrase?

_____

_____

_____

What is the Holy Spirit speaking to
me about this word or phrase?

_____

_____

_____

Where do I feel resistant to this word?

_____

_____

_____

How do I plan to continue to dwell on this today?

_____

_____

_____

Prayer:
Contemplation and rest in his presence
Share your feelings and resistance with God
Thank him for speaking to you

Scripture Read: _____

What word or phrase sticks out to me?

_____

_____

What do I notice about how I feel when reading this word or phrase?

_____

_____

What is the Holy Spirit speaking to me about this word or phrase?

_____

_____

Where do I feel resistant to this word?

_____

_____

How do I plan to continue to dwell on this today?

_____

_____

Prayer:
Contemplation and rest in his presence
Share your feelings and resistance with God
Thank him for speaking to you

Scripture Read: _____

What word or phrase sticks out to me?

_____

_____

What do I notice about how I feel when
reading this word or phrase?

_____

_____

_____

What is the Holy Spirit speaking to
me about this word or phrase?

_____

_____

_____

Where do I feel resistant to this word?

_____

_____

_____

How do I plan to continue to dwell on this today?

_____

_____

Prayer:
Contemplation and rest in his presence
Share your feelings and resistance with God
Thank him for speaking to you

Scripture Read: _____

What word or phrase sticks out to me?

_____
_____

What do I notice about how I feel when reading this word or phrase?

_____
_____
_____

What is the Holy Spirit speaking to me about this word or phrase?

_____
_____
_____

Where do I feel resistant to this word?

_____
_____
_____

How do I plan to continue to dwell on this today?

_____
_____

Prayer:
Contemplation and rest in his presence
Share your feelings and resistance with God
Thank him for speaking to you

Scripture Read: _____

What word or phrase sticks out to me?

_____

_____

What do I notice about how I feel when reading this word or phrase?

_____

_____

_____

What is the Holy Spirit speaking to me about this word or phrase?

_____

_____

_____

Where do I feel resistant to this word?

_____

_____

_____

How do I plan to continue to dwell on this today?

_____

_____

Prayer:
Contemplation and rest in his presence
Share your feelings and resistance with God
Thank him for speaking to you

Scripture Read: _____

What word or phrase sticks out to me?

_____

_____

What do I notice about how I feel when reading this word or phrase?

_____

_____

_____

What is the Holy Spirit speaking to me about this word or phrase?

_____

_____

_____

Where do I feel resistant to this word?

_____

_____

How do I plan to continue to dwell on this today?

_____

_____

Prayer:
Contemplation and rest in his presence
Share your feelings and resistance with God
Thank him for speaking to you

Scripture Read: _____

What word or phrase sticks out to me?

_____

_____

What do I notice about how I feel when
reading this word or phrase?

_____

_____

_____

What is the Holy Spirit speaking to
me about this word or phrase?

_____

_____

_____

Where do I feel resistant to this word?

_____

_____

_____

How do I plan to continue to dwell on this today?

_____

_____

Prayer:
Contemplation and rest in his presence
Share your feelings and resistance with God
Thank him for speaking to you

Scripture Read: _____

What word or phrase sticks out to me?

_____

_____

What do I notice about how I feel when
reading this word or phrase?

_____

_____

What is the Holy Spirit speaking to
me about this word or phrase?

_____

_____

Where do I feel resistant to this word?

_____

_____

How do I plan to continue to dwell on this today?

_____

_____

Prayer:
Contemplation and rest in his presence
Share your feelings and resistance with God
Thank him for speaking to you

Scripture Read: _____

What word or phrase sticks out to me?

_____

_____

What do I notice about how I feel when
reading this word or phrase?

_____

_____

_____

What is the Holy Spirit speaking to
me about this word or phrase?

_____

_____

_____

Where do I feel resistant to this word?

_____

_____

_____

How do I plan to continue to dwell on this today?

_____

_____

Prayer:
Contemplation and rest in his presence
Share your feelings and resistance with God
Thank him for speaking to you

Scripture Read: _____

What word or phrase sticks out to me?

_____
_____

What do I notice about how I feel when
reading this word or phrase?

_____
_____
_____

What is the Holy Spirit speaking to
me about this word or phrase?

_____
_____
_____

Where do I feel resistant to this word?

_____
_____
_____

How do I plan to continue to dwell on this today?

_____
_____

Prayer:
Contemplation and rest in his presence
Share your feelings and resistance with God
Thank him for speaking to you

Scripture Read: _____

What word or phrase sticks out to me?

_____

_____

What do I notice about how I feel when
reading this word or phrase?

_____

_____

_____

What is the Holy Spirit speaking to
me about this word or phrase?

_____

_____

_____

Where do I feel resistant to this word?

_____

_____

_____

How do I plan to continue to dwell on this today?

_____

_____

_____

Prayer:
Contemplation and rest in his presence
Share your feelings and resistance with God
Thank him for speaking to you

Scripture Read: _____

What word or phrase sticks out to me?

_____
_____

What do I notice about how I feel when reading this word or phrase?

_____
_____
_____

What is the Holy Spirit speaking to me about this word or phrase?

_____
_____
_____

Where do I feel resistant to this word?

_____
_____
_____

How do I plan to continue to dwell on this today?

_____
_____

Prayer:
Contemplation and rest in his presence
Share your feelings and resistance with God
Thank him for speaking to you

Scripture Read: _____

What word or phrase sticks out to me?

_____

_____

What do I notice about how I feel when
reading this word or phrase?

_____

_____

_____

What is the Holy Spirit speaking to
me about this word or phrase?

_____

_____

_____

Where do I feel resistant to this word?

_____

_____

_____

How do I plan to continue to dwell on this today?

_____

_____

Prayer:
Contemplation and rest in his presence
Share your feelings and resistance with God
Thank him for speaking to you

Scripture Read: _____

What word or phrase sticks out to me?

_____

_____

What do I notice about how I feel when reading this word or phrase?

_____

_____

_____

What is the Holy Spirit speaking to me about this word or phrase?

_____

_____

_____

Where do I feel resistant to this word?

_____

_____

_____

How do I plan to continue to dwell on this today?

_____

_____

Prayer:
Contemplation and rest in his presence
Share your feelings and resistance with God
Thank him for speaking to you

Scripture Read: _____

What word or phrase sticks out to me?

_____

_____

What do I notice about how I feel when
reading this word or phrase?

_____

_____

_____

What is the Holy Spirit speaking to
me about this word or phrase?

_____

_____

_____

Where do I feel resistant to this word?

_____

_____

_____

How do I plan to continue to dwell on this today?

_____

_____

Prayer:
Contemplation and rest in his presence
Share your feelings and resistance with God
Thank him for speaking to you

Scripture Read: _____

What word or phrase sticks out to me?

_____

_____

What do I notice about how I feel when reading this word or phrase?

_____

_____

What is the Holy Spirit speaking to me about this word or phrase?

_____

_____

Where do I feel resistant to this word?

_____

_____

How do I plan to continue to dwell on this today?

_____

_____

Prayer:
Contemplation and rest in his presence
Share your feelings and resistance with God
Thank him for speaking to you

Scripture Read: _____

What word or phrase sticks out to me?

_____

_____

What do I notice about how I feel when
reading this word or phrase?

_____

_____

_____

What is the Holy Spirit speaking to
me about this word or phrase?

_____

_____

_____

Where do I feel resistant to this word?

_____

_____

How do I plan to continue to dwell on this today?

_____

_____

Prayer:
Contemplation and rest in his presence
Share your feelings and resistance with God
Thank him for speaking to you

Scripture Read: _____

What word or phrase sticks out to me?

_____

_____

What do I notice about how I feel when
reading this word or phrase?

_____

_____

_____

What is the Holy Spirit speaking to
me about this word or phrase?

_____

_____

_____

Where do I feel resistant to this word?

_____

_____

How do I plan to continue to dwell on this today?

_____

_____

Prayer:
Contemplation and rest in his presence
Share your feelings and resistance with God
Thank him for speaking to you

Scripture Read: _____

What word or phrase sticks out to me?

_____

_____

What do I notice about how I feel when
reading this word or phrase?

_____

_____

_____

What is the Holy Spirit speaking to
me about this word or phrase?

_____

_____

Where do I feel resistant to this word?

_____

_____

How do I plan to continue to dwell on this today?

_____

_____

Prayer:
Contemplation and rest in his presence
Share your feelings and resistance with God
Thank him for speaking to you

Scripture Read: _____

What word or phrase sticks out to me?

_____
_____

What do I notice about how I feel when reading this word or phrase?

_____
_____
_____

What is the Holy Spirit speaking to me about this word or phrase?

_____
_____
_____

Where do I feel resistant to this word?

_____
_____
_____

How do I plan to continue to dwell on this today?

_____
_____

Prayer:
Contemplation and rest in his presence
Share your feelings and resistance with God
Thank him for speaking to you

Scripture Read: _____

What word or phrase sticks out to me?

_____

_____

What do I notice about how I feel when reading this word or phrase?

_____

_____

_____

What is the Holy Spirit speaking to me about this word or phrase?

_____

_____

Where do I feel resistant to this word?

_____

_____

How do I plan to continue to dwell on this today?

_____

_____

Prayer:
Contemplation and rest in his presence
Share your feelings and resistance with God
Thank him for speaking to you

Scripture Read: _____

What word or phrase sticks out to me?

_____
_____

What do I notice about how I feel when
reading this word or phrase?

_____
_____
_____

What is the Holy Spirit speaking to
me about this word or phrase?

_____
_____
_____

Where do I feel resistant to this word?

_____
_____
_____

How do I plan to continue to dwell on this today?

_____
_____

Prayer:
Contemplation and rest in his presence
Share your feelings and resistance with God
Thank him for speaking to you

Scripture Read: _____

What word or phrase sticks out to me?

_____

_____

What do I notice about how I feel when
reading this word or phrase?

_____

_____

What is the Holy Spirit speaking to
me about this word or phrase?

_____

_____

Where do I feel resistant to this word?

_____

_____

How do I plan to continue to dwell on this today?

_____

_____

Prayer:
Contemplation and rest in his presence
Share your feelings and resistance with God
Thank him for speaking to you

Scripture Read: _____

What word or phrase sticks out to me?

_____

_____

What do I notice about how I feel when reading this word or phrase?

_____

_____

_____

What is the Holy Spirit speaking to me about this word or phrase?

_____

_____

_____

Where do I feel resistant to this word?

_____

_____

_____

How do I plan to continue to dwell on this today?

_____

_____

_____

Prayer:
Contemplation and rest in his presence
Share your feelings and resistance with God
Thank him for speaking to you

Scripture Read: _____

What word or phrase sticks out to me?

_____
_____

What do I notice about how I feel when reading this word or phrase?

_____
_____
_____

What is the Holy Spirit speaking to me about this word or phrase?

_____
_____

Where do I feel resistant to this word?

_____
_____
_____

How do I plan to continue to dwell on this today?

_____
_____

Prayer:
Contemplation and rest in his presence
Share your feelings and resistance with God
Thank him for speaking to you

Scripture Read: _____

What word or phrase sticks out to me?

_____

_____

What do I notice about how I feel when reading this word or phrase?

_____

_____

_____

What is the Holy Spirit speaking to me about this word or phrase?

_____

_____

_____

Where do I feel resistant to this word?

_____

_____

_____

How do I plan to continue to dwell on this today?

_____

_____

Prayer:
Contemplation and rest in his presence
Share your feelings and resistance with God
Thank him for speaking to you

Scripture Read: _____

What word or phrase sticks out to me?

_____
_____

What do I notice about how I feel when
reading this word or phrase?

_____
_____
_____

What is the Holy Spirit speaking to
me about this word or phrase?

_____
_____
_____

Where do I feel resistant to this word?

_____
_____

How do I plan to continue to dwell on this today?

_____
_____

Prayer:
Contemplation and rest in his presence
Share your feelings and resistance with God
Thank him for speaking to you

Scripture Read: _____

What word or phrase sticks out to me?

_____
_____

What do I notice about how I feel when reading this word or phrase?

_____
_____
_____

What is the Holy Spirit speaking to me about this word or phrase?

_____
_____
_____

Where do I feel resistant to this word?

_____
_____
_____

How do I plan to continue to dwell on this today?

_____
_____

Prayer:
Contemplation and rest in his presence
Share your feelings and resistance with God
Thank him for speaking to you

Scripture Read: _____

What word or phrase sticks out to me?

_____
_____

What do I notice about how I feel when
reading this word or phrase?

_____
_____
_____

What is the Holy Spirit speaking to
me about this word or phrase?

_____
_____
_____

Where do I feel resistant to this word?

_____
_____

How do I plan to continue to dwell on this today?

_____
_____

Prayer:
Contemplation and rest in his presence
Share your feelings and resistance with God
Thank him for speaking to you

Scripture Read: _____

What word or phrase sticks out to me?

_____

_____

What do I notice about how I feel when
reading this word or phrase?

_____

_____

_____

What is the Holy Spirit speaking to
me about this word or phrase?

_____

_____

_____

Where do I feel resistant to this word?

_____

_____

_____

How do I plan to continue to dwell on this today?

_____

_____

Prayer:
Contemplation and rest in his presence
Share your feelings and resistance with God
Thank him for speaking to you

Scripture Read: _____

What word or phrase sticks out to me?

_____

_____

What do I notice about how I feel when reading this word or phrase?

_____

_____

_____

What is the Holy Spirit speaking to me about this word or phrase?

_____

_____

_____

Where do I feel resistant to this word?

_____

_____

_____

How do I plan to continue to dwell on this today?

_____

_____

_____

Prayer:
Contemplation and rest in his presence
Share your feelings and resistance with God
Thank him for speaking to you

Scripture Read: _____

What word or phrase sticks out to me?

_____

_____

What do I notice about how I feel when reading this word or phrase?

_____

_____

What is the Holy Spirit speaking to me about this word or phrase?

_____

_____

Where do I feel resistant to this word?

_____

_____

How do I plan to continue to dwell on this today?

_____

_____

Prayer:
Contemplation and rest in his presence
Share your feelings and resistance with God
Thank him for speaking to you

Scripture Read: _____

What word or phrase sticks out to me?

_____

_____

What do I notice about how I feel when reading this word or phrase?

_____

_____

_____

What is the Holy Spirit speaking to me about this word or phrase?

_____

_____

_____

Where do I feel resistant to this word?

_____

_____

How do I plan to continue to dwell on this today?

_____

_____

Prayer:
Contemplation and rest in his presence
Share your feelings and resistance with God
Thank him for speaking to you

Scripture Read: _____

What word or phrase sticks out to me?

_____

_____

What do I notice about how I feel when reading this word or phrase?

_____

_____

_____

What is the Holy Spirit speaking to me about this word or phrase?

_____

_____

_____

Where do I feel resistant to this word?

_____

_____

_____

How do I plan to continue to dwell on this today?

_____

_____

Prayer:
Contemplation and rest in his presence
Share your feelings and resistance with God
Thank him for speaking to you

Scripture Read: _____

What word or phrase sticks out to me?

_____

_____

What do I notice about how I feel when reading this word or phrase?

_____

_____

_____

What is the Holy Spirit speaking to me about this word or phrase?

_____

_____

_____

Where do I feel resistant to this word?

_____

_____

_____

How do I plan to continue to dwell on this today?

_____

_____

Prayer:
Contemplation and rest in his presence
Share your feelings and resistance with God
Thank him for speaking to you

Made in the USA
Las Vegas, NV
07 April 2023

70337868R00070